To

From

Date

Jesus, without You I am nothing. Thank You for turning my tears into an offering of glory unto Your Name. You are indescribable! Take my life and let it be a sweet fragrant offering unto Thee. I love You!

To the Hunter's Hope Families who have had to say "goodbye" far too soon, yet right on time. I love you all.

And
To my only son,
Hunter.
I miss you. I love you.
And I can't wait to hold you again.

Prayers *for* Those Who Grieve

JILL KELLY

Photography by BRODY WHEELER

HARVEST HOUSE PUBLISHERS

EUGENE, OREGON

Prayers for Those Who Grieve

Text Copyright © 2010 by Jill Kelly
Photography © Brody Wheeler

Published by Harvest House Publishers
Eugene, Oregon 97402
www.harvesthousepublishers.com

ISBN 978-0-7369-2934-9

Design and production by Left Coast Design,
Portland, Oregon

Printed in China

10 11 12 13 14 15 16 / IM / 10 9 8 7 6 5 4 3 2

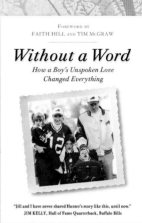

FOREWORD BY
FAITH HILL and TIM McGRAW

Without a Word

*How a Boy's Unspoken Love
Changed Everything*

"Jill and I have never shared Hunter's story like this, until now."
JIM KELLY, Hall of Fame Quarterback, Buffalo Bills

JILL KELLY

For more information on or to purchase Jill Kelly's memoir, *Without a Word*, please visit **www.faithwords.com**. FaithWords is a division of Hachette Book Group.

To the Reader

Before you take this journey, I want to briefly share my heart and hope with you.

As you pour out your intimate cries to the God who loves you and sees you, let the tears fall where they may.

While this book is meant to be a safe haven for all you are wrestling with right now—it's also a dangerous place to let it all out.

A place to let go—and let God.

A place to expose and release the depths of your grief and despair.

Take it with you wherever you go, just in case you find yourself in a moment of mourning that needs expression.

Journaling my thoughts and prayers has been invaluable to my intimate relationship with the Lord. In fact, journaling has allowed me to express tumultuous emotions in a way that has brought deep healing and freedom.

He's listening!

With love, humility, and a bleeding heart on the mend,

Jill Kelly

*Y*ou're probably holding this book in your hands because either you or someone you love is grieving. Before you turn the page, I want you to know how very sorry I am for your loss. If I were standing in front of you right now, my words would be few but my arms would be ready to hug you.

I am grieving too.

My only son, Hunter, was born on his daddy's birthday—Valentine's Day—February 14, 1997. When he was only four months old, our baby boy was diagnosed with a fatal genetic disease that eventually took his precious life eight brief years later.

When I laid my treasured eight-year-old son's lifeless body into the grave, I thought my life was over—and part of it was.

The prayers in this book were taken from the many tearstained pages of several journals I kept during the most agonizing time of my life. In a very real and intimate way, these prayers were part of my healing process. Sharing private moments of mourning with you is not a source of healing for me; it's a result of it.

I am still healing.

Grief is a fragile and intimate process. We all grieve differently, and there are no secret healing formulas, no 12-step recovery programs, and no shortcuts for the grief journey. It is what it is, and it is extremely difficult. Every day we have a choice—will we persevere or cave? While some days life's mundane responsibilities bring a blessed distraction that helps time go by, a gaping hole once filled with joy is now empty. Instead, a relentless, hollow ache echoes through every part of our broken lives.

And it will until heaven.

Time doesn't heal broken hearts or put shattered dreams back together…

Jesus does.

This is a book for the grieving.

A cup to gather your tears.

A resting place where weeping is welcome.

A prayer journey

Through the valley of the shadow of death.

And while this book may be filled with desperate cries, it also overflows with the life-changing, healing hope of God's Word. You may not see or feel Him, but in your darkest days, the Comforter is there.

Though weeping may endure for many nights, a day of great joy will dawn. I know it's hard to imagine ever experiencing real joy again, but I promise you—you will.

Prayers for Those Who Grieve is

    A whisper from the heart of heaven.

        A tender reminder that, when your heart is torn,

            The unfailing grace and love of God holds you.

                Press on, dear friend…

                    You are loved more than you know.

A Simple Prayer for You

Father, You know…

You know the person reading through this prayer book intimately.

You know every hurt…

Every tear…

Every frustration and fear.

You know.

You see.

And You care.

God of compassion and mercy, please reach down
and make a way for healing and restoration.

Please bind up the brokenhearted, free the captive, release the
prisoner, strengthen the weary, and bring hope to the desperate.

Lord, I pray You would turn mourning into
dancing and ashes into beauty.

For the sake of Your name and for Your glory,
please use every tear of anguish and grief.

In a way that only You can, please hold
everyone who needs to be held…

Thank You, Lord.
In the unmatched name of Your beautiful Son, Jesus.

Take Me Too

Lord, please take me too.

The pain is unbearable.

I am drowning in deep anguish, swept away by waves of despair.

Do You see me?

———

I can't

sleep.

I can't

eat.

Everything is

meaningless.

I'm wasting away a little more with every passing day.

Do You hear me, Father?

———

Why does my heart continue to beat?

It's been torn apart and trampled on.

Who stole my life away?

Who can survive this torment called grief?

"My comfort in my suffering is this:
Your promise preserves my life."
—Psalm 119:50

Lord, my God, "though You have made me see troubles,
many and bitter, you will restore my life again; from
the depths of the earth you will bring me up."
—Psalm 71:20

Father, Your Word says, "The God of all grace, who called you to his
eternal glory in Christ, after you have suffered a little while, will
himself restore you and make you strong, firm and steadfast."
—1 Peter 5:10

———

I cling to You and Your Word.

You are

The God who restores and protects.

Without You

I would surely die.

You hear

And see everything.

You know

What I'm going through right now.

You will

Help me to endure.

———

I call to God, and the Lord saves me.
Evening, morning and noon I cry out
in distress, and he hears my voice.

Psalm 55:17

Brokenhearted

Is this what a broken heart feels like?

Is this what it's like to be crushed in spirit?

Lord, is this mourning?

Every breath is a struggle.

The heaviness is suffocating, and

The darkness is very dark.

———

Who will take the pieces of this shattered
life and show me how to live again?

Where is Your light and life, heavenly Father?

When I'm so desperate, why do You seem so distant?

From the depths of my heart I cry out to You, Lord.

My soul cries out for comfort and
restoration from the living God.

———

Save me. Help me to live.

Lift my head off this pillow of
affliction and give me hope.

Revive me, Lord, according to
Your loving-kindness.

Jesus, You promised to comfort those who mourn.

—Matthew 5:4

And turn my mourning into joy and gladness.

—Isaiah 61:1-3

Can real happiness and joy be found again?

It seems impossible.

But You are

The God of the impossible.

Lord, like the psalmist, I long to proclaim that "I am still confident of this: I will see the goodness of the LORD in the land of the living."

—Psalm 27:13

Because You watch over my coming and going both now and forevermore, I will trust You today.

—Psalm 121:8

Although I walk through the valley of the shadow of death, I will fear no evil, because You are with me.

—Psalm 23:4

Your love will sustain and comfort me.

And even though my flesh and heart may fail, You are the strength of my heart and my hope forever.

—Psalm 73:26

During this season of great sadness, Your peace that surpasses all understanding will guard my heart and mind.

—Philippians 4:7

The LORD is close to the brokenhearted and saves those who are crushed in spirit.

Psalm 34:18

Only You Know

You know all things, God.
You know me.
My life is laid bare before You.

You see the confusion and
bitterness clouding my vision.

You hear the whisper of lies
telling me to give up.

You are aware of my darkest fears.

—

My doubts and anxious thoughts
are not a surprise to You.

Even before a word is on my tongue,
You know it completely.
—Psalm 139:4

I pour out the anguish of my soul
before You—because You are safe.

You will not turn away or run from my mourning.

You will never grow tired of hearing me cry.

I don't have to pretend everything is okay
When it's not.

I don't have to pull myself together
When I'm completely broken.

You love me right now.

In the midst of this mess of grief, You love me.

—

Even when I doubt You, Your promises carry me.

As deep as this pit of despair goes—
You, O Lord, are deeper still.

You give strength to the weary
and increase the power of the weak.
—Isaiah 40:29

And after I have suffered a little while, You will
restore me and make me strong, firm, and steadfast.
— 1 Peter 5:10

—

Jesus, You know!

*You were despised, rejected, a man
of sorrows, and familiar with grief.*
—Isaiah 53:3-4

*Thank You for leaving the paradise
of heaven to come down and rescue
a desperate and hurting world.*

*Thank You, Lord, for loving us enough to
endure agony beyond comprehension.*

Thank You for the hope we have in eternal life.

My soul clings to You because

You know.

O Lord, you have searched me
and you know me. You know when
I sit and when I rise; you perceive
my thoughts from afar.

Psalm 139:1-2

It's Okay

Who can live like this?

Life seems so empty and meaningless.

I feel hollow and lost.

Where can I find life and hope?

Everywhere I look I am reminded of what used to be.

Not a day goes by that I don't ponder the life and love of yesterday.

———

I miss _____.

I miss everything about him/her.

———

Is it okay to feel this way?

Am I going to be okay?

Will our family survive?

Life will never be the same.

Is it supposed to be?

I feel so vulnerable.

Help me, Lord, to be still and know that You are God.
> *—Psalm 46:10*

You are greater than my heart, and You know everything.
> *—John 3:20*

Though now each day is sown in tears, a day will come when I will reap with songs of joy.
> *—Psalm 126:5*

It's hard to believe joy will come but it will—

Because

You promised.
> *—Psalm 30:5*

And You are faithful

To all Your promises and

Loving toward all You have made.
> *—Psalm 145:13*

God is our refuge and strength,
an ever-present help in trouble…
"Be still and know that I am God."
> *Psalm 46:1,10*

A Little Bit Longer

In just a little while everything will be okay.

For our life is but a breath here on earth—a fleeting shadow that quickly fades.

—*Psalm 144:4*

"There is a time for everything, and a season for every activity under heaven: a time to be born and a time to die…a time to weep and a time to laugh, a time to mourn and a time to dance."

—*Ecclesiastes 3:1-9*

Even though it's extremely hard to understand, there is a time for everything—even a time to die.

———

Your ways and thoughts are higher, beyond understanding. Who can fully know You or figure You out?

—*Isaiah 55:8-9*

Life and every single breath are in Your hands.

—*Job 12:10*

Your sovereign mercy covers all creation. There is life in Your presence.

_____'s life is still in Your hands.

He/she is very much alive in Your presence right now.

Knowing that Your love covers me while I wait gives me overwhelming comfort.

———

Jesus, thank You for making it possible for me to press on.

Thank You for the hope I cling to—I will see _____ again!

Without You I would have no hope

For tomorrow.

Without You I would have no hope

To persevere today.

I will not grieve as one who has no hope, for my hope is in You and the many promises You have made.

—*1 Thessalonians 4:13*

In just a little while I will see You face-to-face.
—Revelation 22:4

Until that day, please help me to live for
You.

Even in the midst of my grief, allow my life

To be a beacon of faith.

Shine the amazing light of Your truth

Through my pain.

So that all will see

And know that

You

Are God.

Use every tear

I have cried.

Thank You for holding me as I wait

Just a little bit longer.

Therefore we do not lose
heart. Though outwardly we are
wasting away, yet inwardly we are
being renewed day by day. For our
light and momentary troubles
are achieving for us an eternal
glory that far outweighs
them all.

2 Corinthians 4:16-17

Longing for More

This world has nothing
I desire.
My heart longs for more.

—

I'm just going through the motions
Of life.
Pretending is exhausting.
If I could, I would run away—far away.

I wish I could run away from myself.
I don't like who I am right now.

—

The weight of carrying around this heavy heart is
   crippling.
My tears have been my food both day and night.
   —Psalm 42:3
Will I always be so sad?
I can't help it. I can't just move on.

No one understands.

It's life as usual all around me.

I need help.

I need more faith, more assurance.

I need more of You.

Who understands and knows me like You do?

You breathe life into me and fulfill the purpose for my existence.
   —*Acts 17:25*

You hold the keys of life and death.
   —*Revelation 1:18*

Eternity belongs to You.

You have placed a longing for eternity in my heart.
   —*Ecclesiastes 3:11*

Please replace the lies with truth and cover me
   with Your Word.

Your Word is life!

You are the more

That I long for, Jesus,

Right now

And

Forever…

I cry out to God Most High, to God,
who fulfills His purpose for me.

Psalm 57:2

Where Do I Go from Here?

Heavenly Father, I am desperate

To hear from You.

Why do You seem so far away when I am so anxious

For Your presence?

"Hear my prayer, O LORD, listen to my cry for help; be not deaf to my weeping."
—Psalm 39:12

This barrenness is draining.

I feel so…

Alone.

Please come, Lord.

Come and fill this emptiness with Your presence.

Come and fill my heart with life and love again.

The despair of loss is so destructive.

Nothing seems to matter anymore.

I feel lost and hopeless.

But I am not alone during this season of grief.

You will carry me until I see Your face.

When it seems as though I have filled the ocean with tears…

More come.

———

Where do I go from here? Show me the way, Lord.

You are my Shelter and Refuge.

I run to You. With all the strength I can muster

I run.

I surrender all, right now.

I give up! Because I have nothing left to give.

You are my hope.

You are my strength and my Deliverer.
  —*Psalm 144:2*

Hold me together.

Hold my family together through this season of
  grief.

Carry me, Father. And in a very real, tangible way,

Allow me to feel

Your touch.

"Reach down your hand from on high; deliver me
and rescue me."
  —*Psalm 144:7*

I have nothing to give. But I have

YOU!

O God, you are my God, earnestly
I seek you; my soul thirsts for you,
my body longs for you, in a dry and
weary land where there is no water.

Psalm 63:1

Even When
My Faith Fails

O Lord, hear my prayer, listen to my cry for mercy;
in your faithfulness and righteousness come to my relief."

—Psalm 143:1

My faith is being tested, Lord.

All I have trusted in and held on to

Is being shaken.

———

Why am I being bombarded

With fear and doubt?

Why am I questioning

The very faith that has sustained me thus far?

My faith and hope in You alone

Has sustained me through the darkest valleys.

And yet, even now my heart is torn

With uncertainty and confusion.

The enemy of my soul is trying to steal everything.

—John 10:10

But You, Lord, have given me life.

My hope is in You.

Your Word stands true forever.

—*1 Peter 1:25*

I am held.

You go before me and will be with me; You will never leave me nor forsake me. I will not be afraid or discouraged. I will be strong and courageous.

—*Deuteronomy 31:8*

YOU WILL NEVER FAIL ME!

As deep as this pit of doubt goes, Your love and mercy are deeper still.

You are not absent

During this time of weeping.

Even when my faith fails, in Your faithfulness

Nothing and no one can tear me from Your grasp.

—John 10:28-29

When I can't hold on, You hold me.

—Colossians 1:17

"Find rest, O my soul, in God alone; my hope comes from him. He alone is my rock and my salvation; He is my fortress, I will not be shaken."

—Psalm 62:6

Although my heart and my faith and even my flesh may fail, You will never fail me. You are the strength of my heart and my portion forever.

—Psalm 73:26

I will press on with the measure of faith You have given me.

I will live and endure by faith and not by sight Lord, for Your hand will guide me.

—2 Corinthians 5:7

You are my life! Thank You, Lord.

We fix our eyes not on what is seen,
but on what is unseen. For what is seen is
temporary, but what is unseen is eternal.

2 Corinthians 4:18

I lift up my eyes to the hills—
where does my help come from?
My help comes from the
LORD, the Maker of
heaven and earth.

Psalm 121:1-2

Where Does My Help Come From?

Father, I'm going to die

If You leave me here.

If You leave me in this treacherous storm

I will surely drown.

Who can survive such anguish?

Come quickly, Lord, and save me!

Please take this cup of suffering from me.

———

I need You!

I can't do this. I can't bear this weight of grief.

Please take me.

Take me away!

I am tired, scared, weak, frustrated, and downcast.

Where is my hope?

———

Can peace

Be found in the midst of this storm?

Please scoop me up

And put me in a safe place

Away from this torment,

Away from the enemy.

My help comes from You, Lord.

You are with me.

You will deliver me.

———

I will not fear the terror of night, for You are my dwelling place.

—Psalm 91

"I will lie down and sleep in peace, for You alone, O Lᴏʀᴅ, make me dwell in safety."

—Psalm 4:8

I cry out to You, Lord, in my trouble, and You alone will bring me out of my distress. You will still this storm to a whisper.

—Psalm 107:28-29

———

Thank You, Lord, for Your unfailing love, hope, and mercy.

In You, Jesus, peace is found. In this world I will have trouble.

But my hope is in You and I take heart

Because You

Have overcome the world.

—John 16:33

Without You

As life ebbs away with each passing day...

Where is my hope?

Will it ever get better?

"I am bowed down and brought very low; all day long I go about mourning."

—*Psalm 38:6*

Will this heaviness ever be lifted?

———

I feel as though I am already dead.

I can't seem to fight the battle waged against me nor escape it.

Keep me strong until the end, Lord.

Free me from this yoke, this bondage, this oppression, this stronghold.

Even my very eyes are dim with despair.

"I am feeble and utterly crushed; I groan in anguish of heart. All my longings lie open before you, O LORD; my sighing is not hidden from you. My heart pounds, my strength fails me; even the light has gone from my eyes."

—*Psalm 38:8-10*

———

Without You I have nothing.

Without You I am nothing.

Your greatness is unsearchable.

You are beyond comprehension.

Your thoughts and ways are higher than my thoughts and my ways.
—*Isaiah 55:8*

When I don't understand You, I choose

To trust You.

—

Who can fathom Your grace and majesty?

You uphold all who fall and lift up all who are bowed down.
—*Psalm 145:14*

You will keep me strong until the end…

Until the day of Christ Jesus.
—*1 Corinthians 1:8*

And after I have suffered a little while, You will restore me and make me strong, firm, and steadfast.
—*1 Peter 5:10*

The Lord is righteous
in all his ways and loving
toward all he has made.
Psalm 145:17

While I Wait

$\mathcal{E}$veryday is

one

day

closer.

———

Today is one day closer to You, Lord,

To heaven.

To eternity.

To _____ again.

———

As each day passes, I wait.

Some days I'm not very patient.

In fact, I'm just frustrated and

Anxious, longing for what's to come.

I long for a glimpse of heaven, just

A glimpse.

How long will this season last?

———

Thank You for the hope I have in all You have
promised.

Thank You for preparing a place for me while I wait
to see Your face.
  —*John 14:2*

Please, Lord,

I pray You would be enough

While I wait.

———

You know my heart.

You know my thoughts and fears.

Fill my heart and mind with more of You.

Help me to be heavenly minded and earthly good.

Bind up my wounded heart in Your life and love.

While I wait

Help me to live.

Bless me with an undivided
And captivated heart
Focused on You
While I wait.

I will be in Your presence someday.
I can't even imagine.
My soul sings with tears
While

I

wait.

Help me to hope again.

Bring back the joy of my salvation and lead me

In the way everlasting.

Fill the emptiness as I cling to You for everything.

Let every breath I take praise You

Especially now

In my grief.

Strengthen me

While I wait.

I say to myself, "The LORD is my portion; therefore I will wait for him"…it is good to wait quietly for the salvation of the Lord.

Lamentations 3:24-26

Beautiful

You have made everything beautiful in its time.
—*Ecclesiastes 3:11*

Are my tears beautiful to You, Lord?

Will You take the despair that consumes me and make it beautiful?

Are You still enthralled with my beauty?
—*Psalm 45:11*

———

I don't feel very beautiful.

What do You see when I look in the mirror?

I don't like what I see.

I see discouragement and fear

Weariness of heart and soul.

I see brokenness and bitterness

Despair and death.

I see a woman struggling to live another day.

I see mourning.

And yet, in the midst of grief and darkness I see You.

I see Your beauty.

I see how You alone have come to bind up the brokenhearted, to proclaim freedom for the captives and release from darkness for the prisoner.
—*Isaiah 61:1*

I am not a prisoner or captive during this season of mourning. I am free.

Free to be sad.

Free to be

Who I am in this process.

Free to be

Who You created me to be.

———

You have come to comfort all who mourn, provide for those who grieve and bestow a crown of beauty instead of ashes—the oil of gladness instead of mourning and a garment of praise instead of a spirit of despair.
—*Isaiah 61:3*

While I mourn and grieve…

You will comfort me.

Joy and gladness will return because of Your compassion and faithfulness.

In the midst of this sorrow, You are worthy to be praised.

Somehow, the beauty of Your suffering has made the suffering of Your children beautiful.

Sounds crazy.

How can anything good come from suffering?

The cross!

You are amazing, Jesus!

You're beautiful.

There is a time for everything,
and a season for every activity under
heaven: a time to be born and a time
to die…a time to mourn and a time
to dance…He has made everything
beautiful in its time.

Ecclesiastes 3:1-11

Where Else Can I Go?

As far as the east is from the west

You are there.

As high as the heavens and to the depths of the raging seas

You are there.

In the quietness of my heart where deep pain and longings dwell

You are there.

In grief

You are there.

In the midst of deep suffering

You are there.

Who can hide from You?

You are everywhere. I can't run from You…

You see me.

You see all of me.

Everything is laid bare before You.

You know the depths of who I am and You still

Love me.

———

Lord, You're amazing.

My hope is in You and Your
Word today and forever.
  —*Psalm 119:114*

Where else can I go? Whom do I have in heaven and on earth but You? And earth has nothing I desire besides You.
  —*Psalm 73:25*

You are the way, the truth, and the life.
  —*John 14:6*

You hold the keys to eternity.

You are forever!

You see the unseen and hear the unspoken.

The multitudes of heaven worship You alone.

———

And I am Yours. I'm not my own.

My life is in Your hands.

I belong to You.

All that I am I surrender to You. I'm nothing
without You.

You are the light that brightens this darkened
path.

You are the whisper of hope when everything falls
apart.

You take the shattered pieces of brokenness and
create something beautiful.

Thank You, Lord.

Lord, sustain me as you promised
that I may live! Do not let
my hope be crushed.

Psalm 119:116 NLT

Free

What comfort I have in knowing that

I am free.

In this prison of mourning and grief

Freedom can still be found.

"Turn to me and be gracious to me, for I am
lonely and afflicted. The troubles of my heart
have multiplied; free me from my anguish."
  —*Psalm 25:16-17*

Only in Your presence are the wounded and
    afflicted comforted

And the sick made well.

Though my tears have been my food both day
    and night…

I am free.

———

There is freedom in knowing who I am in You,
    Lord.

There is freedom in knowing You.

I don't have to run away from the pain of deep
    sorrow.

I don't have to pretend that I'm okay.

I don't have to try and look good in the midst of
    this darkness.

Because You are my strength and song

I am free.

———

Though countless eyes watch me as I journey
    through the rain

You love me.

And that's all I need to know. I don't have to prove anything.

I have nothing left to give.

I'm empty.

My life has been poured out.

I don't have to try and hold myself together because

You hold me.

I'm devastated and yet I have hope because

I have You.

My confidence is

In You.

Thank You for setting me free.

Your truth has set me free.

In my anguish I cried to the
LORD, and he answered
by setting me free.

Psalm 118:5

Remember

O heavenly Father, help me remember all You have done.

Help me to remember You.

In the midst of this sorrow, help me to remember Your faithfulness.

Write the truth of who You are on my heart.

Hide Your promises and the hope of heaven deep within my soul.

Fill my life with memories of _____ and Your faithfulness throughout our journey together.

I long to remember.

As each day passes—the memories drift so far away.

 seems so far away.

I long to hold his/her frail body again and touch his/her soft skin.

I know he's/she's in better hands now—he's/she's in Your hands.

But my hands long to touch him/her again.

———

While I wait—Lord, please help me to remember.

Help me to remember the joy.

Lord, even in the midst of suffering, profound joy and peace can be experienced.

Thank You for revealing Yourself in so many real and tangible ways.

Do it again, Lord.

Fill our lives with Your joy and peace even now

As we remember You and all You have done.

Lord, when we forget, as we often do, please nudge our hearts toward You

And help us

To remember.

"On my bed I remember you; I think of you through the watches of the night. Because you are my help, I sing in the shadow of your wings. My soul clings to you; your right hand upholds me."

—*Psalm 63:6-8*

I will remember the deeds of the
LORD; yes I will remember your
miracles of long ago. I will meditate
on all your works and consider
all your mighty deeds.

Psalm 77:11-12

Save Me

Save me, O God, for the floodwaters are up to my neck. Deeper and deeper I sink into the mire; I can't find a foothold to stand on. I am in deep water, and the floods overwhelm me. I am exhausted from crying for help; my throat is parched and dry. My eyes are swollen with weeping, waiting for my God to help me.

—Psalm 69:1-3

How long, Lord?

How long will my heart beat in anguish?

When will the waves of despair cease from trying to pull me under?

No one understands…

…why do I expect them to?

You're the only one I can run to.

You're the only one who can still the raging storm within my soul.

———

Save me from myself.

Release me from expectations

Only You can fill.

Revive me and deliver me…

Turn your ear to me and save me.

"Be my rock of refuge, to which I can always go."
—Psalm 71:2

Please, God, rescue me!

Come quickly, Lord, and help me.
—Psalm 70:1

I drink in tears by the bowlful…

Where are You?

———

Hear my heart when words don't make any sense.

Is this normal, Lord? Is anything "normal" when it comes to grief?

Restore me, O God; make Your glorious face shine down upon me and my family, that we may be saved.

—*Psalm 80:3*

Lord, please preserve my life, my marriage, my family.

"I have suffered much; preserve my life, O LORD, according to your word."

—*Psalm 119:107*

Here I am, Lord.

I trust You to save me and rescue me from this storm.

O LORD, the God who saves me,
day and night I cry out before you.
May my prayer come before you;
turn your ear to my cry.

Psalm 88:1-2

Trying to Find My Way

or my soul is full of trouble and my life draws near the grave."

—Psalm 88:3

Life is a vapor...here today and gone tomorrow.

—James 4:14

Teach me to number my days, Lord, that I may gain a heart of wisdom.

—Psalm 90:12

Someday life here will come to an end.

Until then, help me to live.

Help me to press on when I don't understand.

Help me to trust You every step on this journey.

Keep me focused on You when my eyes are dim with grief.

"I call to You, O LORD, every day; I spread out my hands to you."

—Psalm 88:9

———

When You took _____, You took part of me.

Part of my flesh and blood is in heaven with You right now.

As I journey through life without _____, I cling to You.

Without You, I would surely lose my way.

This road is hard and treacherous, piercing my soul at every turn.

"My heart is sick, withered like grass, and I have lost my appetite...My life passes as swiftly as the evening shadows."

—Psalm 102:4,11 NLT

———

Yet Your love and faithfulness surround me.

I walk in the light of Your presence, O Lord.

Your peace has swept over me.

You are my hiding place.

I run to You, Lord.

In You

I find myself.

In You,

I find my way.

You

Are the way.

Then they cried out to the LORD
in their trouble, and he brought them
out of their distress. He stilled the
storm to a whisper; the waves
of the sea were hushed.

Psalm 107:28-29

There Is Hope

I'm screaming as loud as I can, but

No one is

Listening.

Does anyone hear

Me crying?

"I am worn out from groaning; all night long I flood my bed with weeping and drench my couch with tears. My eyes grow weak with sorrow."
—Psalm 6:6-7

Help!

———

I feel so alone.

Have You abandoned me?

Why are You silent?

Never in all my life have I felt

So downcast

    So afraid

       So lifeless

         So damaged.

"Turn to me and be gracious to me, for I am lonely and afflicted. The troubles of my heart have multiplied; free me from my anguish. Look upon my affliction and my distress."
—Psalm 25:16-18

Where are You, Jesus?

———

"Listen to my prayer, O God, do not ignore my plea; hear me and answer me. My thoughts trouble me and I am distraught."
—Psalm 55:1-2

Painful thoughts overwhelm me day and night.

"My heart is in anguish within me; the terrors of death assail me. Fear and trembling have beset me; horror has overwhelmed me. I said, 'Oh, that I had the wings of a dove! I would fly away and be at rest—I would fly far away and stay in the desert; I would hurry to my place of shelter, far from the tempest and storm.' "
—Psalm 55:4-8

Please take me away and deliver me from this torment.

I feel like a prisoner in my own flesh.

If I could, I would run away from myself.

Can I escape the sorrow of my soul?

Can the hardened ground of my heart be tilled and nourished?

This road is treacherous and unfamiliar. But there is hope.

"I cry out to God Most High, to God, who fulfills his purpose for me. He sends from heaven and saves me...God sends his love and his faithfulness."
   —Psalm 57:2-3

Your love protects and heals.

"In God, whose word I praise...in God I trust; I will not be afraid."
   —Psalm 56:10-11

Help me to fully trust in what I cannot see. You are present even when I can't feel Your presence.

Even though my flesh and heart may fail, You are the strength of my heart and my portion forever.
   —Psalm 73:26

Show me the wonder of who You are.

You have delivered me from
death and my feet from stumbling,
that I may walk before God
in the light of life.

Psalm 56:13

How Long?

I am so weary.

My heart is crushed and the pain

Is overwhelming.

I'm sad.

This is so hard.

My soul cries out for comfort, for restoration, for direction, for help.

I'm completely undone.

"How long, O Lord? Will you forget me forever? How long will you hide your face from me? How long must I wrestle with my thoughts and every day have sorrow in my heart? How long will my enemy triumph over me? Look on me and answer, O Lord my God. Give light to my eyes, or I will sleep in death."

—Psalm 13:1-3

Lord, please…

From the depths of my heart I cry out to You.
I'm trying to find my way.

The road is rough.

My heart is broken.

Despair is lurking nearby.

Will I stand or fall?

Break down or be strong?

Will this pain ever cease?

"Be merciful to me, LORD, for I am faint; O LORD, heal me, for my bones are in agony. My soul is in anguish. How long, O LORD, how long? Turn, O LORD and deliver me; save me because of your unfailing love."

—*Psalm 6:1-4*

Lift my head.

Gently place Your mighty, tender hands under my chin and

Raise my head heavenward.

Turn my mourning into dancing and my sorrow into joy, for I have put my hope in You.

Let the tears wash away the scales from my eyes so I can see You.

Reveal Yourself in the midst of this pain, Lord.

———

Help me to take every thought captive and make it obedient to Christ.

—*2 Corinthians 10:5*

I will not fear, for You are with me always.

—*Deuteronomy 31:8*

Your promises are true and they will stand forever.

Help me to live

To breathe

To hope again.

———

I long for better days.

Revive me.

You are my Rock, my Fortress, and my Deliverer…

My Shield and my Stronghold.

—*Psalm 18:2*

You are my only hope.

He reached down from on high and took hold
of me; he drew me out of deep waters. He rescued
me from my powerful enemy...the LORD was my
support. He brought me into a spacious place;
he rescued me because he delighted in me.

Psalm 18:16-19

Love Endures

What great pain this love has caused me.

And yet how full the joy for having loved so hard

And so deep.

There's nothing like it.

A love that endures forever.

———

There's no greater gift than to have loved
and be loved unconditionally.

And there's no greater pain than to let go
of the one who was loved so completely.

What is love without pain?

Is there such a thing?

———

Love hurts.

And sometimes the pain is unbearable.

I find it hard to keep breathing, to keep waiting.

My heart is torn.

Help me to endure.

Help me to look to Your sacrifice and rest in Your love.

How blessed I am to have experienced a love beyond comprehension.

What a gift!

And to know and believe that I don't have to be afraid to love again.

"There is no fear in love. But perfect love drives out fear."
     —1 John 4:18

O Lord, my fears disappear in the swell of Your immeasurable love.

A love that endures forever.

———

We love because you first loved us.
     —1 John 4:19

You are love.

My love is made complete in You alone.

Your love covers me.

Your love strengthens me.

Your love helps me to breathe and live again.

———

Because Your love endures forever, I have hope.

Great is his love toward us,
and the faithfulness of the
LORD endures forever.

Psalm 117:2

Precious in Your Sight

While grief is my daily companion, I seek You.

During this season of heartbreak, I cling to You.

"You, O Lord, have delivered my soul from death,
my eyes from tears, my feet from stumbling."
—Psalm 116:8

What would I do without You?

———

You fill my emptiness.

And keep me safe.

Your compassion and mercy are abundant.

And Your love unchanging.

———

My tears are precious to You.

You see me.

You hear me.

And in my dismay, You hold me.

"I love the Lord, for he heard my voice;
he heard my cry for mercy. Because he turned
his ear to me, I will call on him as long as I live."
—Psalm 116:1-2

In Your hands I find rest.

In Your love I find hope.

Because of You I live.

———

You are my everything.

I need You.

You will not forget me.

My life and love are hidden in You alone.

———

"Send forth your light and your truth, let
them guide me; let them bring me to your holy
mountain, to the place where you dwell."
—Psalm 43:3

Because of You I will survive.

Because of You my loss has meaning.

And I have hope.

Precious in the sight of the
LORD is the death of
his saints.

Psalm 116:15

Heaven

Though every day here is a gift, we are not home yet.

Heaven is our real home.

I long for a glimpse of heaven…

———

I can't even imagine

And often ponder what paradise is like.

Are children sitting at Your feet, wide eyed

With awe and wonder?

Are Your beloved dancing and singing with hands held high?

Who can stand in the glory

Of Your beauty?

Are Your precious children face down

Extending their crowns toward Your throne?

What's it like?

What do they see?

What do they feel?

What do they hear?

Your Word proclaims that the multitudes of heaven worship You.
—Nehemiah 9:6

_____ is now part of that glorious multitude.

Knowing that he/she is with You right now overwhelms me with hope and anticipation. Thank You, Lord!

The heavens declare Your awesome glory and the skies proclaim the work of Your hands.
—Psalm 19:1

You're amazing!

———

You have placed a longing for eternity in our hearts, Lord.
—Ecclesiastes 3:11

This world and all its treasures are meaningless

Compared to the greatness of knowing You.

No wonder we long for more.

All creation groans for Your return.

How long will You wait to rescue Your beloved?

———

"Now we see but a poor reflection as in a mirror; then we shall see face to face. Now I know in part; then I shall know fully, even as I am fully known."
—1 Corinthians 13:12

The tapestry of life You have so graciously woven together

Will make sense.

What we have hoped for

Will finally come to be.

There is great comfort in knowing that the grave is not the end.

In heaven, there is no more death or mourning or crying or pain. All of our tears will be wiped away and the old order of things has passed away.
—Revelation 21:4

No more sickness, disease, and sin.

Nothing will hurt in heaven.

There is no confusion or chaos

Just peace.

And freedom.

_____ is free!

What our hearts have desired from the day of our birth

Will become a reality.

Every tear I have cried

Will pour forth as a beautiful offering

For Your glory and praise.

Wow…

The greatest gift in heaven is You, Jesus.

You are what heaven is all about.

Do not let your hearts be
troubled. Trust in God; trust
also in me. In my Father's house
are many rooms; if it were not so,
I would have told you. I am going
there to prepare a place for you.
And if I go and prepare a place
for you, I will come back and
take you to be with me that
you also may be where I am.

John 14:1-3

Acknowledgments

"I thank my God every time I remember you. In all my prayers for all of you, I always pray with joy because of your partnership in the gospel from the first day until now, being confident of this, that He who began a good work in you will carry it on to completion until the day of Christ Jesus. It is right for me to feel this way about all of you, since I have you in my heart" (Philippians 1:3-7).

With sincere thanks and deep gratitude…

To my mother, Jacque. Your unconditional love and deep passion inspire me to be more like Jesus.

To my husband, Jim. Your encouragement has meant more than words can say. God is so good. Thank you for praying daily for my "writings"! To my daughters, Erin and Camryn. I thank God for both of you. I love you so much. You shine like the stars in the heavens. I'm so proud to be your mother. Thank you for reading through Mommy's prayers; you are both gifted writers and editors.

To my tenderhearted nephew, Benjamin. I thank God for you and your love for His creation. I'm especially grateful for your passion for nature. I pray that God will increase your desire to know Him through all He has created. Love you, Ben!

To my dear friend "Maverick," editor extraordinaire. Rick, you are a blessing. Thank you for being a constant "Barnabas." I know God has allowed our paths to cross "for such a time as this."

To the Harvest House team—Bob, LaRae, Jean, Kim, and Jeff. It has been a blessing to be able to work alongside all of you to bring this heart-drenched book to all who need it. God is so good!

To Robert Wolgemuth and the entire team at Wolgemuth & Associates. You are an extraordinary group. I'm so grateful God has brought us together. Your encouragement and patience has meant so much to me. I hope ours is a lifelong journey of serving God together.